D1540891

How to Improve Concentration and Focus

10 Exercises and 10 Tips to Increase Concentration

by Vivian Sandau

Table of Contents

Introduction

We live in a golden technological era – and things will only get "better" from here. The constant exposure to a never-ending chatter of social media feeds, games, videos, movies, YouTube; the ease of communication, which ensures that anyone we want to contact can be reached in a matter of seconds, through text, voice or video chat; the itchy urge to dig deeper into the smallest, most random thought that may pop into our heads, thanks to the magic of Google; the 1,000-odd channels that most of us receive on our telev-idiot-box; the 1,073,775,000 websites (and counting; yes, I Googled it) on the internet, catering to every store of knowledge, taste, fetish, or even idle curiosity, and available in a matter of seconds at the touch of a few buttons. All of it basically points to a single fact: It's so **bloody** difficult to concentrate on the task at hand, in the face of these (titanic x leviathan)^raised to Mount Everest sized distractions.

The end result? Most people today have the attention span and focus of a hyper-caffeinated squirrel chomping down on methamphetamines like tic tacs. We hop from unfinished project to unfinished project, flit around piled-up work by giving in to any one of these easily accessible diversions at the drop of a hat, and so on and so forth – until we're left with ever increasing piles of work and ignored responsibilities, and basically as much control over our minds as a junkie going through withdrawal.

This systematic and unending devotion to fulfilling our smallest whims then ends up degrading our focus and productivity until we have the attention span of a gnat, plays merry hell with our short-term memory and observational powers, and leaves us with as much internal calm and serenity as a burning forest in a post-nuclear apocalypse.

But instead of playing slave to our minds, we can wrest back that lost control through a series of simple tips and exercises, to be practiced every day. After all, curiosity is an excellent trait – in moderation – and if we bend our minds to our will, instead of the other way around, we can amp up productivity, focus, etc., while achieving a calmer mental state. And **that** is the purpose of this book! So, are you ready to delve into these secrets, new and old, and gain control back over your mind from these never-ending distractions? Let's get started!

Exercise 1: Practice Mindfulness

The speed at which most of us jet through our daily lives today guarantees that we (a) no longer stop and smell the flowers and (b) do not fully appreciate the experiences to which we devote our time.

If you disagree with me, I can prove it to you with a few questions:

1) If you're with a partner, can you recall a time when one of you confessed your feelings to the other? If so, can you recall what the sky looked like, or how the breeze felt, in that moment? Can you recall all the smells, sounds and sights – in short, every sensory experience in that indubitably important moment – around you at that point of time? Or how hard your heart was thumping, or whether your mouth felt dry?

2) Can you recall what you had for breakfast five days ago? Or three? If you had a fruit, do you remember what that fruit looked like? I mean, specifically, that particular fruit, not the generic image from that family of fruits that just popped into your head. Can you remember distinctly how that one smelled? Whether it smelt and looked delicious? Was it ripe, raw, sweet, or sour? Did it have any marks or dents on it? Can you remember the same for whatever you had for lunch yesterday? (If your head just countered with "pshah, but it's just a fruit. What do I care?" you've already lost this round)

All of us eat, work, sleep, travel, exercise, get intimate – all of it in a rush. We no longer take the time to devote our minds entirely to the senses involved in the task at hand – instead, we devote our minds to wandering around taxes, fees, bills, that movie we wanted to watch, problems, issues, etc.

This is where Mindfulness is an applicable exercise. Mindfulness is essentially a Buddhist philosophy which espouses the *here* and the *now*. It embraces each experience, whether professional or personal, and advocates devoting all your senses to that experience.

If you enjoy cooking, don't put shows on in the background, or think about problems while you cook – instead, devote your mind to each sight, sound, feeling and sizzle around you while performing the task. Concentrate on the smell and feel of your ingredients while you chop them, memorize each textural change that occurs in the process, devote your sight and attention to each pop and sizzle on the pan.

Similarly, if you're jogging – devote your senses to the feel of your feet thumping on the road, smell the air around you and feel the breeze through which you run, concentrate on the sounds of your beating heart and those of your surroundings, instead of simply listening to the latest thumping and jarring beats on your iPod.

Mindfulness has been established as a practice which not only increases concentration, focus, and observational prowess, but also makes each task infinitely more wholesome, memorable, and joyous.

8

While many arenas of your life may require multi-tasking for better time management, you need to remember – just like simultaneous multi-dating dilutes the emotional impact and connection of each of the bonds among the people involved, so does multi-tasking devolve your bond with any of the tasks you perform. Consequently, you are neither performing your best – giving your all to any of the tasks you're juggling – nor deriving any pleasure from any of the tasks involved, because you're busy trying to manage time like a robot. There are activities that you perform every day in which you can avoid multi-tasking and practice mindfulness instead. Slowly, but surely, those observational practices will become effortless for you; no matter how busy your life may be, or how many tasks you may need to rush through.

Exercise 2: Practice Stillness

Staying still is the hardest thing for anyone in this modern jungle. And, before any of you retorts with "but we don't have time," even the President of the United States, or the CEO of a Fortune 500 company, manages to make some time every day to devote to their own leisure – even if it's just 5 or 10 minutes in a day. Watch one less YouTube video in a day, and presto! You've made time for this exercise.

The point of this exercise is very simple: Find a comfortable spot in a chair, couch, or even your bed; situate yourself in a comfortable position that you can maintain for 10-15 minutes – and then just stay still. Simple, isn't it? Not as simple as you think. You'll See, You'll All See! [Evil Maniacal Laugh]

Set a timer for 15 minutes. Once you start, devote all your attention to not making a single movement. Stay absolutely still. You'll notice that not doing anything takes a lot more effort and concentration than actually doing something. Once you feel like you're starting to grasp the basics of this, feel the room around you – listen to the sounds inside and outside your house. You can even pretend you're a superhero with super-hearing and try and strain your ears to pick up the smallest or quietest sounds around you. Whatever you do, Do Not Move.

After a few days, you should find that staying still is getting easier and easier for you to maintain – but do not let other thoughts intrude upon this time. This is not a time for you to hash out other problems in your head – it's simply a time to do and think about absolutely nothing.

Once you get the hang of this, not only will you start feeling more refreshed after you're done every day, but you'll also find that learning with cognitive reasoning may seem easier. After all, if people are over-filled pots of water, constantly running around and sloshing their contents all over the place whenever they struggle with learning something new, then this exercise is the equivalent of throwing out all the water, while still retaining all the knowledge – it empties your mind for another fresh bout of mental struggles.

Exercise 3: Breathing Exercises

Before you mock this exercise, keep in mind that eastern cultures and philosophies have embraced the regulation of one's breath as the first step towards conquering an unruly mind for millennia.

There are plenty of ancient philosophical systems which state that there is a direct correlation between the number of breaths one takes and one's lifespan, or between the quality of one's inner energy and the regulation and discipline of one's breathing.

Our goals here, however, are slightly more scientific and vastly less spiritual. Deep breathing infuses your blood with more oxygen, which better oxygenates your brain and thus promotes a clearer and sharper mind.

This exercise is better known in yogic terms as "Pranayama," and is an ancient breathing exercise which is, to this day, widely followed in Southeast Asian cultures.

Let me clarify that you don't need to sit cross-legged or otherwise for this exercise – as discussed above, just find a comfortable spot.

You start with holding your right hand over your nose (as if you're going to pinch it closed). Gently press on the right side of your nose with your thumb to block that nostril, then breathe in through your left nostril while counting to three (1 Mississippi, 2 Mississippi,...). Next, close both nostrils by pinching your nose with your index finger and thumb, then hold your breath in for another count of three. Finally, lift your thumb off your right nostril and expel your breath slowly to the count of three.

Repeat the exercise by continuing to keep your left nostril closed and breathing in through your right nostril for a count of three; and so on and so forth, as I'm sure you get the basic idea.

Repeat this exercise for 10 to 15 minutes every day, once or twice a day.

Exercise 4: Start Learning a New Language

Studies have already proven that multilingual people are able to concentrate and reason through cognitive processes better and faster than those who aren't able to employ multiple languages. Additionally, studies have shown that a problem you may be grasping with may be easier to solve when repeating the circumstances to yourself in a foreign language.

There are more e-books and apps (e.g. Duolingo) than I care to count, which would make this an easy, fast, convenient, and immensely fun process for you. And there are absolutely zero side-effects to learning a new language (except open-mindedness, acceptance, tolerance, and a deeper understanding of the world and its diverse cultures – absolutely horrible, I know).

Having to process thought and speech patterns in multiple languages also makes your mind more aware, and by the time you're able to juggle multiple languages effortlessly, your concentration and focus will have improved exponentially.

For those of you who are saying "But I already know two/three/a few languages," the title of the exercise instructs you to "learn a new one!" It may also help you improve your ability to read, and to interpret what you're reading.

Like any other stimulus, a language with which you've been intimately familiar for a while now will jog your brain a lot less than a fresh stimulus, such as a new language.

Exercise 5: If You Have Time to Play Farmville, You Have Time to Play Memory Games!

You should've already understood what this section is about. There are a myriad of memory apps and games available on the Google Play Store, or available for purchase and download elsewhere on the Internet.

All you need is five minutes a day; choose from apps like Brain Age Test, Lumosity, CogniFit, etc., and just play a few rounds each day. Different apps concentrate on different areas of memory and concentration, although there are some (paid or free) which are pretty comprehensive as well. They're fun, addictive, and distracting in the glorious tradition of pretty much everything else around us today; but immensely productive and beneficial at the same time.

These apps vastly improve your short-term memory, do wonders for your concentration and, like all great games, simultaneously ignite a competitive fire in you to do better on their scoreboards.

Exercise 6: Dexterity Exercises

Some of the dexterity exercises given by medical practitioners or therapists to people who may have suffered a wrist or hand injury – in order to rehabilitate and improve neurological or muscular control in that area – serve pretty well in improving focus and concentration.

This is a pretty simple exercise to follow, and will not only improve the dexterous control of your fingers, but will help you focus as well.

You can perform this exercise anywhere – literally – and don't need to practice it for longer than five minutes a day.

Perform this exercise simultaneously with both hands.

All you need to do is to touch each fingertip with the tip of your thumb of the same hand. You start by touching the tip of your thumb (not the nail) to the tip of your little finger, then to your ring finger's tip, then the middle finger, and lastly the index finger. You need to make sure that you're touching the tips and not the middle or anywhere else on the finger. You continue this by going back to touch the tip of your little finger with the tip of your thumb, and repeating the entire thing over and over again for the duration of the exercise.

This can be especially helpful if you're in a lecture or meeting and find it difficult to concentrate, or find yourself getting distracted. Do this exercise a few times, until you feel you're back in the here-and-now, and able to focus on what's in front of you.

Another helpful tip in such a situation, if you're unable to do the finger exercises but are unable to concentrate, may be simply wiggling your toes. Often, when we need to sit for longer stretches of time, we either start feeling restless, or start daydreaming – essentially signals from the body or mind that it wants to be anywhere other than where it is, and doing anything other than what it's doing at the moment. Wiggling your toes gives you some motion and respite from that restlessness, and may ease up on your body's or mind's need for distraction long enough to be able to wrest its attention back to the present.

Exercise 7: Talk to the Mirror

This exercise not only helps with focus and concentration, but also serves as a self-empowerment tool and builds confidence in oneself.

You don't need to practice this for more than three to five minutes each day.

Stand in front of a mirror and relax yourself a little. Use a marker or a lipstick to draw two eyes around your own reflection's eyes in the mirror, as if those were the eyes of someone with whom you were talking.

Keep your sight fixed within those eyes on the mirror, and don't let your gaze wander. Don't think about anything else. Instead, feel the sensations in and around you as you keep your gaze fixed. Breathe deeply and keep meeting the eyes in the mirror.

Once you've done this for a while, you'll find it a lot easier to concentrate on different sensations in and around you without inadvertently averting your gaze from the mirror. Once your gaze is effortlessly fixed on the mirror, use your peripheral vision to notice your own facial muscles and structure in the mirror. You can even smile slowly and see (and feel) the way your muscles move as you form a smile (still through the edges of your vision, without moving your gaze away from the eyes in the mirror).

After a few days practicing this exercise, you'll notice that your observational powers are growing in leaps and bounds, that you're more aware of your peripheral vision, and that you're significantly more confident while talking to other people.

While you continue practicing this exercise, and keeping your gaze firmly on the eyes in the mirror, you can also practice working on your posture, as is visible through the edges of your vision. This is an incredible exercise to promote physical self-awareness. Do not let your thoughts get polluted with imagined or mentally exaggerated insecurities or false misgivings about your appearance while you're undertaking this exercise. Keep your mind empty of thoughts, and flood it with feelings and sensations instead.

Exercise 8: Focus on Your Own Body

This particular exercise improves focus, concentration, attention span, and muscle control.

For this exercise, it's best to lie down comfortably and set aside a duration of thirty minutes. Alternately, instead of doing this during the day, you can attempt it before sleeping and so make it a part of your bed-time ritual.

Once you're in bed, lie on your back and spread your arms and legs slightly apart from your body so as to occupy a comfortable amount of space. Keep your hands relaxed with your palms facing upwards. Once you're in this position, just lie still and count to sixty while taking deep breaths. Pay attention to every sensation and feeling in your body, and don't think about anything else. If any thought seems to be intruding, simply remind yourself that this takes top priority for the moment and that anything else can wait for a little bit. Push the distraction gently aside from your mind and return to the task at hand.

Once you've counted to sixty, slowly start wiggling the toes on one foot – and nothing else – for a count of thirty. Focus your attention on the toes alone, and make sure no other part of your body moves. Feel the way your muscles shift in your foot when you're wiggling your toes, and the way the air feels when your toes are moving through it. Then switch to the toes on the other foot and do the same. Embrace and concentrate on the sensations in your body as you make an individual part move, while keeping the rest of your body as still as possible.

Once you're done with the toes, move to the ankles of each foot – first moving them so that your foot moves back and forth towards and away from you, then rotating your ankle in a slow, controlled, circular motion. Make sure you regulate your breathing all throughout the exercise.

After you're done with your ankles, move to your knees, then your hips, your fingers, your wrists, your elbows, your shoulders, your neck, and then all the way back down to your toes again.

While this may take a little time, this exercise will greatly improve your ability to concentrate on the task at hand, give you a renewed appreciation for your body, and relax you greatly before bedtime so that you can sleep soundly.

Exercise 9: Self-Policing

Human beings are masters of self-delusion and deception. Our minds are layered with so many self-defense mechanisms that it becomes quite difficult for us to understand and correct our own flaws. Thus, the most important thing for us to do is to stop defending our errors and face up to them, instead of cowering and running away, fearful of shattering our carefully constructed lies about ourselves.

The most efficient and least painstaking way for us to concentrate and focus better on the task at hand is to open our own eyes as to how deep-seated the problem really is, and how often it seems to show up.

The easiest way to do this is with a piece of paper that we can carry around with us. Every day, before you leave for your office, studies, etc., take a piece of paper and a pen and be sure to carry it around with you. Every time you feel like you're getting distracted from the task at hand, simply put a tick mark on the paper. You can divide this sheet into three sections – morning, afternoon and evening – if it feels like this would enable you to understand your behavior better. Alternatively, you can note the time beside each tick.

Every night, just glance at the piece of paper and take note of how many ticks there are. You don't even need to save the paper. You could just as easily throw it away after taking a careful look at it. After all, you're unlikely to forget the barrage of tick marks filling up the page.

After a few days, you'll notice that you're automatically correcting yourself if you seem to be getting distracted, and that the paper is getting far less populated with tick marks than when you started.

The simple reason for this is that we hate flaws within ourselves. While we aren't presented with absolute proof on the matter, we try to explain them away, camouflage them, or try to debunk the messenger that is pointing out our flaws. But with self-policing, we know every mark on that paper to be accurate – and it takes a frighteningly lazy and self-deluding person indeed to ignore the evidence that they themselves have compiled.

Exercise 10:   Read One Long Article or Short eBook per Day

The worst thing in our generation to happen to curiosity and bountiful stores of knowledge all across the world is the birth of the TL;DR (Too Long; Didn't Read) culture. There has never before been such a wide-spread and prodigious attempt at covering up stupidity with "coolness."

It's also one of the most frightening symptoms of the attention span problems that I've been trying to highlight throughout this guide. A recent survey has shown that 24% of Americans haven't read a single book in the past year. If you don't quite understand why that's frightening, you should spend some of your "Google time" trying to gain a better appreciation of the history of books, printing, the spread of knowledge, before and after mass availability, relations between curiosity and reading, correlations between IQ, taste, and number of books read, etc.

If you want to rein in that unruly mind, find some sites that specialize in long articles (they offer everything from humor to politics, etc.) and spend 10 minutes a day reading just *one* long article, if you can't manage more than that.

Not only will this improve your information retention, short-term memory, focus, attention span, and concentration, it will vastly improve your knowledge and expose you to pleasures that you had never before experienced. It will also make you more patient and inquisitive, and provide for you a better appreciation of toiling at something in order to receive its full benefits.

Conclusion

Out of all the possible problems that may plague the human mind, lack of concentration and focus are, by far, the *easiest* to solve; yet, they are the ones that people crib and whine about the most, and over which they constantly procrastinate. Compare yourself to someone who has a neurological disorder and loses control over his/her memory, concentration, and focus, with no hope for the situation to be reversible. People like that often work tirelessly to keep their minds sharp through the exercises that I've outlined in this guide and more; and yet, they would *literally* give up an arm or a leg to be in your shoes – i.e. lacking focus and concentration simply because you couldn't be bothered to work on it.

Your mind, and its functions, can be successfully equated to any other muscle in your body – if you stop exercising it productively, it atrophies. The steps discussed in this guide don't take a lot of time, or effort for that matter, and make a massive difference in whether you're able to be a productive, high-performing, curious, intelligent, and aware member of society.

Beside the exercises outlined in the guide, these tips that you should carry with you are as simple as they are effective.

1. Separate your working space from your sleeping space. Preferably, work from a table. On its own, it improves focus and productivity.

2.   Get regular and sufficient amounts of sleep. A tired brain is unable to send impulses along its neural pathways as efficiently as it would when well-rested. If you think pulling all-nighters and surviving on a pittance of sleep is somehow making you a better worker, you're sorely mistaken.

3.   Exercise – at your desk, through seated crunches, if nothing else. Regular exercise greatly improves blood flow, which enables higher brain functions, thus giving you a sharper mind. After all, no bodily function is exclusive and independent of the others.

4.   Practice meditative techniques, or do yoga every day. These reduce unnecessary stress, which is a well known force for lack of focus.

5.   Try to finish whatever you start – be it a project, game, book, etc. You need to discipline your brain and enforce the understanding that constantly flitting from one half-formed thought to another is unacceptable.

6.   If you understand your largest distractions well, clear your working space of any and all of them.

7.   Give your brain a break, after every 45 minutes or hour-long period of work, when you start working

on your focus. The brain performs best during refreshed sprints rather than labored marathons. However, keep trying to increase the time that you can work at a single stretch, since it usually takes the brain about 15-20 minutes to fully return to the task at hand once it is distracted.

8. Mindfulness is more than an exercise – it's a philosophy, which you should abide by. You can practice easily enough when you're walking to the store to buy groceries, or while cleaning your house.

9. Most of the reparations to be done in your brain are concerned with memory, rather than focus alone. The more often you challenge your brain with memory games, the easier you'll find the rest of the exercises as well.

10. If you want to improve focus and concentration, think of yourself as Sherlock Holmes while out on a walk – if that helps you. Just as no detail, no matter how big or small, would escape the famed detective – so should nothing escape your piercing, hawk-like gaze. (Disclaimer: This point is not to be used as an excuse to creepily ogle strangers.)

Finally, I'd like to thank you for purchasing this book! If you enjoyed it or found it helpful, I'd greatly appreciate it if you'd take a moment to leave a review on Amazon. Thank you!

Made in the USA
Lexington, KY
05 June 2017